Name of Business ______________
For Tax Year ________
Employer Identification Numbers
Federal ______________
State ____________________

Small Business Made Simple

Small Business Payroll System Simplified

by Daniel Sitarz
Attorney-at-Law

Nova Publishing Company
Small Business and Consumer Legal Books and Software
Carbondale, Illinois

Editorial assistance by Janet Harris Sitarz, Linda Jorgensen-Buhman, and Melanie Bray. Interior design by Linda Jorgensen-Buhman. Manufactured in the United States.

ISBN 0-935755-55-1 Book only ($14.95)

Cataloging-in-Publication Data
Sitarz, Dan, 1948-
Small Business Payroll System Simplified / by Daniel Sitarz. -- 1st ed.
128 p. cm. -- (Small Business Made Simple series).
1. Payroll—United States—Popular Works. 2. Payroll—United States—Forms.
3. Payroll—United States—States—Popular Works. I. Sitarz, Daniel.
II. Title. III. Series.
ISBN 0-935755-55-1, Book only ($14.95).

Nova Publishing Company is dedicated to providing up-to-date and accurate legal information to the public. All Nova publications are periodically revised to contain the latest available legal information.

1st Edition; 1st Printing December, 2003

This publication is designed to provide accurate and authoritative information in regard to the subject matter covered. It is sold with the understanding that the publisher and author are not engaged in rendering legal, accounting, or other professional services. If legal advice or other expert assistance is required, the services of a competent professional person should be sought.

—From a Declaration of Principles jointly adopted by a Committee of the American Bar Association and a Committee of Publishers

DISCLAIMER

Because of possible unanticipated changes in governing statutes and case law relating to the application of any information contained in this book, the author, publisher, and any and all persons or entities involved in any way in the preparation, publication, sale, or distribution of this book disclaim all responsibility for the legal effects or consequences of any document prepared or act on taken in reliance upon information contained in this book. No representations, either express or implied, are made or given regarding the legal consequences of the use of any information contained in this book. Purchasers and persons intending to use this book for the preparation of any legal documents are advised to check specifically on the current applicable laws in any jurisdiction in which they intend the documents to be effective.

Nova Publishing Company
Small Business and Consumer Legal Books and Software
1103 West College Street
Carbondale, IL 62901
Editorial: (800) 748-1175

Distributed by:
National Book Network
4501 Forbes Blvd.
Lanham, MD 20706
Orders: (800) 462-6420

Table of Contents

Payroll Forms

This payroll workbook was designed to simplify the preparation of weekly payroll and the required monthly, quarterly, and annual federal and state payroll tax filings. In addition to this book, you will need a number of other federal and state forms to complete your payroll. Federal forms are available from the IRS by phone: 1(800)TAX-FORM or by download: www.irs.gov

IRS Form SS-4: Application for Employer Identification Number: This form must be filed before you begin to hire and pay any employees.
IRS Form W-4: Employee's Withholding Allowance Certificate: This form should be filled out by each employee and also by continuing employees whose personal situation has changed.
BCIS Form 1-9: Employment Eligibility Verification: This immigration form is required of all employees and can be downloaded at www.bcis.gov
IRS Circular E (Publication 15): Employer's Tax Guide: This booklet is necessary to determine the amounts that must be withheld from employees' pay for federal income tax, Social Security and Medicare. (There may also be updated withholding tables available from the IRS that may be required).
IRS Form 940: Employer's Annual Federal Unemployment Tax (FUTA) Return: Required to be filed annually by all employers if they pay wages of over $1,500.00 in any quarter or have any employee for over 20 weeks.
IRS Form 941: Federal Quarterly Return of Withholding, Social Security, and Medicare Taxes: Required of all employees who have employees subject to withholding taxes.
IRS Form 8109: Federal Tax Deposit Coupon: To be used by any employer with a monthly federal withholding tax liability over $500.00.
IRS Form W-2: Wage and Tax Statement: Required to be filed with the IRS and provided to each employee annually.
IRS Form W-3: Transmittal of Wage and Tax Statements: Required to be filed with the IRS annually accompanying the filing of employee W-2 statements.
State and Local forms: There may be various forms that are required for the payment of state and local income and/or unemployment taxes. Contact the local or state taxing authority directly.

Instructions for Using Payroll Records

Upon Hiring An Employee

① Have employee complete *IRS Form W-4* and *BCIS Form I-9.*
② Enter employee's name, address, phone, date hired, Social Security #, and rate of pay on *Employee Records* sheet.

For Each Week of Payroll

① Enter date of week on *Employee Payroll Records* sheet.
② Enter names of each employee for that week in first column and their marital status and withholding allowance amount in next columns.
③ For each employee, enter hours worked for each day and total. Enter overtime hours and rate if applicable.
④ Multiply number of hours worked by rate of pay and enter in *Gross Pay* column.
⑤ Determine federal income tax, Social Security tax, Medicare (from *IRS Circular E*) and any state or local deductions. Total all deductions and subtract from *Gross Pay*. Enter amount under *Net Pay* and prepare employee paycheck for net pay amount.
⑥ After completing payroll for all employees, carry amounts over to *Cumulative Quarterly Totals* columns. *Note*: After the first payroll week, you will need to add each new week's totals to the prior week's *Cumulative Totals*. *Note:* You can fold the *Employee Payroll Records* sheet where indicated to simplify this task.

At the End of Each Month

① Complete all weekly payroll tasks.
② Turn to the *Quarterly Payroll Depository Record* page for the appropriate quarter.
③ At the end of the month, enter the current month's totals for all federal income tax withheld from all employees (this amount can be found by totaling the *Federal Tax* column in your current *Cumulative Quarterly Totals* on the *Employee Payroll Records* sheet).
④ Also enter totals for employee's share of Social Security and Medicare taxes. These amounts can also be found in your current *Cumulative Quarterly Totals* on the *Employee Payroll Records* sheet.
⑤ Enter an equal amount for the employer's share of Social Security and Medicare taxes in the appropriate columns on the *Quarterly Payroll Depository Record. Note*: The employer matches the employee's withholding amounts for Social Security and Medicare.
⑥ Calculate totals for the month, enter amount in *Total Deposit* column, and make payment for this amount to your bank using *IRS Form 8109.*

At the End of Each Quarter

① Complete all monthly payroll tasks.
② Carry all amounts from your final *Cumulative Quarterly Totals* column on your weekly *Employee Payroll Record* sheets to the appropriate *Quarterly Employee Payroll Summary* sheet.
③ Total the amounts on your *Quarterly Payroll Depository Record* and use these amounts to complete and file *IRS Form 941.*
④ On the appropriate *Quarterly State Unemployment Contribution Record*, enter each employee's name and total quarterly net pay amount. Total all net pay and multiply by your state's unemployment multiplier rate (available from your state). Use these amounts to complete your state's *Quarterly Unemployment Insurance Tax Return* (also available from your state).

At the End of the Year

① Complete all quarterly payroll tasks for the fourth quarter.
② On the *4th Quarter and Annual Employee Payroll Summary* sheet, carry totals over from first three quarters and enter at bottom of form. Total these columns for your annual totals.
③ On the *4th Quarter and Annual Payroll Depository Record* sheet, carry totals over from first three quarters and enter at bottom of form. Total these columns for your annual totals.
④ On the *4th Quarter and Annual State Unemployment Contribution Record* sheet, carry totals over from first three quarters and enter at bottom of form. Total these columns for your annual totals.
⑤ You will use all of your annual totals to complete your final annual payroll tax filings: *IRS Form 940*; *IRS Form W-2*; *IRS Form W-3*; and any annual state or local payroll tax returns.

EMPLOYEE RECORDS

Employee Name	Address	Phone	Date Hired	Date Ended	Social Security Number	Starting Pay Rate

EMPLOYEE PAYROLL RECORDS

Pay Period Ending: July 18, 20 04

Employee Name	Married or Single	Withholding Allowances	Hours Worked M	T	W	Th	F	Sa	Su	Total Regular Hours	Overtime Hours / Overtime Rate	Hourly Rate of Pay	Gross Pay	
Sue Murphy	M	2	8	8	8	8	8	8		40	8 / 15.00	10.00	520	00
Bill Walsh	M	4	8	0	8	8	8			32	0	9.00	288	00
Joan Allen	S	1	6	6	6	6	6			30	0	7.00	210	00
Nancy Smith	S	0	2	3	1	6	1			13		6.00	78	00
John Jones	M	1	2	0	2	0	2			6		6.00	36	00
Totals for Period			26	17	25	28	25	8		121	8		1132	00

EMPLOYEE PAYROLL RECORDS

WITHHOLDING AND DEDUCTIONS							CUMULATIVE QUARTERLY TOTALS						
Federal Tax	Social Security	Medicare	State Tax	Other	Total Deduction	Net Pay	Gross Pay	Federal Tax	Social Security	Medicare	State Tax	Other	Net Pay
25 00	32 24	7 54	15 60		80 38	439 62	1500 00	75 00	96 72	22 62	46 80		1,258 86
0 00	17 86	4 18	8 64		30 68	257 32	864 00	0 00	53 58	12 54	25 92		771 96
10 00	13 02	3 05	6 30		32 37	177 63	630 00	30 00	39 06	9 15	18 90		532 89
3 00	4 84	1 13	2 34		11 31	66 69	234 00	9 00	14 52	3 39	7 02		200 07
0 00	2 23	52	1 08		3 83	32 17	108 00	0 00	6 69	1 56	3 24		96 51
38 00	70 19	16 42	33 96	0 00	158 57	973 43	3336 00	114 00	210 57	49 26	101 88	0 00	2860 29

FOLD

EMPLOYEE PAYROLL RECORDS

Pay Period Ending: ______________________ , 20 _____

Employee Name	Married or Single	Withholding Allowances	Hours Worked M	T	W	Th	F	Sa	Su	Total Regular Hours	Overtime Hours / Overtime Rate	Hourly Rate of Pay	Gross Pay	
Totals for Period														

EMPLOYEE PAYROLL RECORDS

WITHHOLDING AND DEDUCTIONS							CUMULATIVE QUARTERLY TOTALS						
Federal Tax	Social Security	Medicare	State Tax	Other	Total Deduction	Net Pay	Gross Pay	Federal Tax	Social Security	Medicare	State Tax	Other	Net Pay

FOLD

EMPLOYEE PAYROLL RECORDS

Pay Period Ending: ______________________ , 20 _____

Employee Name	Married or Single	Withholding Allowances	Hours Worked							Total Regular Hours	Overtime Hours / Overtime Rate	Hourly Rate of Pay	Gross Pay	
			M	T	W	Th	F	Sa	Su					
Totals for Period														

EMPLOYEE PAYROLL RECORDS

WITHHOLDING AND DEDUCTIONS							CUMULATIVE QUARTERLY TOTALS						
Federal Tax	Social Security	Medicare	State Tax	Other	Total Deduction	Net Pay	Gross Pay	Federal Tax	Social Security	Medicare	State Tax	Other	Net Pay

FOLD

EMPLOYEE PAYROLL RECORDS

Pay Period Ending: ______________________ , 20 _____

Employee Name	Married or Single	Withholding Allowances	Hours Worked							Total Regular Hours	Overtime Hours / Overtime Rate	Hourly Rate of Pay	Gross Pay	
			M	T	W	Th	F	Sa	Su					
Totals for Period														

EMPLOYEE PAYROLL RECORDS

WITHHOLDING AND DEDUCTIONS							CUMULATIVE QUARTERLY TOTALS						
Federal Tax	Social Security	Medicare	State Tax	Other	Total Deduction	Net Pay	Gross Pay	Federal Tax	Social Security	Medicare	State Tax	Other	Net Pay

FOLD

EMPLOYEE PAYROLL RECORDS

Pay Period Ending: ______________________ , 20 _____

Employee Name	Married or Single	Withholding Allowances	Hours Worked							Total Regular Hours	Overtime Hours / Overtime Rate	Hourly Rate of Pay	Gross Pay	
			M	T	W	Th	F	Sa	Su					
Totals for Period														

EMPLOYEE PAYROLL RECORDS

WITHHOLDING AND DEDUCTIONS							CUMULATIVE QUARTERLY TOTALS						
Federal Tax	Social Security	Medicare	State Tax	Other	Total Deduction	Net Pay	Gross Pay	Federal Tax	Social Security	Medicare	State Tax	Other	Net Pay

FOLD

EMPLOYEE PAYROLL RECORDS

Pay Period Ending: ______________________ , 20 _____

Employee Name	Married or Single	Withholding Allowances	Hours Worked							Total Regular Hours	Overtime Hours / Overtime Rate	Hourly Rate of Pay	Gross Pay	
			M	T	W	Th	F	Sa	Su					
Totals for Period														

EMPLOYEE PAYROLL RECORDS

WITHHOLDING AND DEDUCTIONS							CUMULATIVE QUARTERLY TOTALS						
Federal Tax	Social Security	Medicare	State Tax	Other	Total Deduction	Net Pay	Gross Pay	Federal Tax	Social Security	Medicare	State Tax	Other	Net Pay

FOLD

EMPLOYEE PAYROLL RECORDS

Pay Period Ending: ______________________ , 20 _____

Employee Name	Married or Single	Withholding Allowances	Hours Worked M	T	W	Th	F	Sa	Su	Total Regular Hours	Overtime Hours / Overtime Rate	Hourly Rate of Pay	Gross Pay	
Totals for Period														

EMPLOYEE PAYROLL RECORDS

WITHHOLDING AND DEDUCTIONS							CUMULATIVE QUARTERLY TOTALS						
Federal Tax	Social Security	Medicare	State Tax	Other	Total Deduction	Net Pay	Gross Pay	Federal Tax	Social Security	Medicare	State Tax	Other	Net Pay

FOLD

EMPLOYEE PAYROLL RECORDS

Pay Period Ending: ______________________ , 20 ____

Employee Name	Married or Single	Withholding Allowances	Hours Worked M	T	W	Th	F	Sa	Su	Total Regular Hours	Overtime Hours / Overtime Rate	Hourly Rate of Pay	Gross Pay	
Totals for Period														

EMPLOYEE PAYROLL RECORDS

WITHHOLDING AND DEDUCTIONS							CUMULATIVE QUARTERLY TOTALS						
Federal Tax	Social Security	Medicare	State Tax	Other	Total Deduction	Net Pay	Gross Pay	Federal Tax	Social Security	Medicare	State Tax	Other	Net Pay

FOLD

EMPLOYEE PAYROLL RECORDS

Pay Period Ending: ______________________ , 20 _____

Employee Name	Married or Single	Withholding Allowances	Hours Worked							Total Regular Hours	Overtime Hours / Overtime Rate	Hourly Rate of Pay	Gross Pay	
			M	T	W	Th	F	Sa	Su					
Totals for Period														

EMPLOYEE PAYROLL RECORDS

WITHHOLDING AND DEDUCTIONS							CUMULATIVE QUARTERLY TOTALS						
Federal Tax	Social Security	Medicare	State Tax	Other	Total Deduction	Net Pay	Gross Pay	Federal Tax	Social Security	Medicare	State Tax	Other	Net Pay

FOLD

EMPLOYEE PAYROLL RECORDS

Pay Period Ending: ______________________ , 20 _____

Employee Name	Married or Single	Withholding Allowances	Hours Worked M	T	W	Th	F	Sa	Su	Total Regular Hours	Overtime Hours / Overtime Rate	Hourly Rate of Pay	Gross Pay	
Totals for Period														

EMPLOYEE PAYROLL RECORDS

WITHHOLDING AND DEDUCTIONS							CUMULATIVE QUARTERLY TOTALS						
Federal Tax	Social Security	Medicare	State Tax	Other	Total Deduction	Net Pay	Gross Pay	Federal Tax	Social Security	Medicare	State Tax	Other	Net Pay

FOLD

EMPLOYEE PAYROLL RECORDS

Pay Period Ending: ______________________ , 20 _____

Employee Name	Married or Single	Withholding Allowances	Hours Worked M	T	W	Th	F	Sa	Su	Total Regular Hours	Overtime Hours / Overtime Rate	Hourly Rate of Pay	Gross Pay
Totals for Period													

EMPLOYEE PAYROLL RECORDS

WITHHOLDING AND DEDUCTIONS							CUMULATIVE QUARTERLY TOTALS						
Federal Tax	Social Security	Medicare	State Tax	Other	Total Deduction	Net Pay	Gross Pay	Federal Tax	Social Security	Medicare	State Tax	Other	Net Pay

FOLD

EMPLOYEE PAYROLL RECORDS

Pay Period Ending: ______________________ , 20 _____

Employee Name	Married or Single	Withholding Allowances	Hours Worked M	T	W	Th	F	Sa	Su	Total Regular Hours	Overtime Hours / Overtime Rate	Hourly Rate of Pay	Gross Pay	
Totals for Period														

EMPLOYEE PAYROLL RECORDS

WITHHOLDING AND DEDUCTIONS							CUMULATIVE QUARTERLY TOTALS						
Federal Tax	Social Security	Medicare	State Tax	Other	Total Deduction	Net Pay	Gross Pay	Federal Tax	Social Security	Medicare	State Tax	Other	Net Pay

FOLD

EMPLOYEE PAYROLL RECORDS

Pay Period Ending: ______________________ , 20 _____

Employee Name	Married or Single	Withholding Allowances	Hours Worked M	T	W	Th	F	Sa	Su	Total Regular Hours	Overtime Hours / Overtime Rate	Hourly Rate of Pay	Gross Pay	
Totals for Period														

EMPLOYEE PAYROLL RECORDS

WITHHOLDING AND DEDUCTIONS							CUMULATIVE QUARTERLY TOTALS						
Federal Tax	Social Security	Medicare	State Tax	Other	Total Deduction	Net Pay	Gross Pay	Federal Tax	Social Security	Medicare	State Tax	Other	Net Pay

FOLD

EMPLOYEE PAYROLL RECORDS

Pay Period Ending: ____________________ , 20 ____

Employee Name	Married or Single	Withholding Allowances	Hours Worked: M	T	W	Th	F	Sa	Su	Total Regular Hours	Overtime Hours / Overtime Rate	Hourly Rate of Pay	Gross Pay	
Totals for Period														

EMPLOYEE PAYROLL RECORDS

WITHHOLDING AND DEDUCTIONS							CUMULATIVE QUARTERLY TOTALS						
Federal Tax	Social Security	Medicare	State Tax	Other	Total Deduction	Net Pay	Gross Pay	Federal Tax	Social Security	Medicare	State Tax	Other	Net Pay

FOLD

EMPLOYEE PAYROLL RECORDS

Pay Period Ending: ______________________ , 20 _____

Employee Name	Married or Single	Withholding Allowances	Hours Worked M	T	W	Th	F	Sa	Su	Total Regular Hours	Overtime Hours / Overtime Rate	Hourly Rate of Pay	Gross Pay	
Totals for Period														

EMPLOYEE PAYROLL RECORDS

WITHHOLDING AND DEDUCTIONS							CUMULATIVE QUARTERLY TOTALS						
Federal Tax	Social Security	Medicare	State Tax	Other	Total Deduction	Net Pay	Gross Pay	Federal Tax	Social Security	Medicare	State Tax	Other	Net Pay

FOLD

1st QUARTER EMPLOYEE PAYROLL SUMMARY

Quarter Ending: ______________________ , 20 _____

Employee Name	Gross Pay	Federal Income Tax	Social Security	Medicare	State Tax	Other	Net Pay
Totals for Quarter							

1st QUARTER PAYROLL DEPOSITORY RECORD

Month	Federal Inome Tax		Employee Share Social Security		Employer Share Social Security		Employee Share Medicare		Employer Share Medicare		Total Deposit	
Quarterly Total												
Cumulative Total												
Total Number of Employees for Quarter:												

1st QUARTER STATE UNEMPLOYMENT CONTRIBUTION RECORD

Employee Name	Total Quarterly Net Pay		Employee Name	Total Quarterly Net Pay	
Total Net Pay for This Column			Total Net Pay for This Column		
			Total Net Pay for All Employees (both columns)		
			x State Unemployment Multiplier Rate		
			= Total Quarterly Unemployment Due		

EMPLOYEE PAYROLL RECORDS

Pay Period Ending: ______________________ , 20 _____

Employee Name	Married or Single	Withholding Allowances	Hours Worked							Total Regular Hours	Overtime Hours / Overtime Rate	Hourly Rate of Pay	Gross Pay	
			M	T	W	Th	F	Sa	Su					
Totals for Period														

EMPLOYEE PAYROLL RECORDS

WITHHOLDING AND DEDUCTIONS							CUMULATIVE QUARTERLY TOTALS						
Federal Tax	Social Security	Medicare	State Tax	Other	Total Deduction	Net Pay	Gross Pay	Federal Tax	Social Security	Medicare	State Tax	Other	Net Pay

FOLD

EMPLOYEE PAYROLL RECORDS

Pay Period Ending: ______________________ , 20 _____

Employee Name	Married or Single	Withholding Allowances	Hours Worked M	T	W	Th	F	Sa	Su	Total Regular Hours	Overtime Hours / Overtime Rate	Hourly Rate of Pay	Gross Pay	
Totals for Period														

EMPLOYEE PAYROLL RECORDS

WITHHOLDING AND DEDUCTIONS							CUMULATIVE QUARTERLY TOTALS						
Federal Tax	Social Security	Medicare	State Tax	Other	Total Deduction	Net Pay	Gross Pay	Federal Tax	Social Security	Medicare	State Tax	Other	Net Pay

FOLD

EMPLOYEE PAYROLL RECORDS

Pay Period Ending: ____________________ , 20 ____

Employee Name	Married or Single	Withholding Allowances	Hours Worked M	T	W	Th	F	Sa	Su	Total Regular Hours	Overtime Hours / Overtime Rate	Hourly Rate of Pay	Gross Pay	
Totals for Period														

EMPLOYEE PAYROLL RECORDS

WITHHOLDING AND DEDUCTIONS							CUMULATIVE QUARTERLY TOTALS						
Federal Tax	Social Security	Medicare	State Tax	Other	Total Deduction	Net Pay	Gross Pay	Federal Tax	Social Security	Medicare	State Tax	Other	Net Pay

FOLD

EMPLOYEE PAYROLL RECORDS

Pay Period Ending: ______________________ , 20 _____

Employee Name	Married or Single	Withholding Allowances	Hours Worked							Total Regular Hours	Overtime Hours / Overtime Rate	Hourly Rate of Pay	Gross Pay	
			M	T	W	Th	F	Sa	Su					
Totals for Period														

EMPLOYEE PAYROLL RECORDS

WITHHOLDING AND DEDUCTIONS							CUMULATIVE QUARTERLY TOTALS						
Federal Tax	Social Security	Medicare	State Tax	Other	Total Deduction	Net Pay	Gross Pay	Federal Tax	Social Security	Medicare	State Tax	Other	Net Pay

FOLD

EMPLOYEE PAYROLL RECORDS

Pay Period Ending: ______________________ , 20 ____

Employee Name	Married or Single	Withholding Allowances	Hours Worked							Total Regular Hours	Overtime Hours / Overtime Rate	Hourly Rate of Pay	Gross Pay	
			M	T	W	Th	F	Sa	Su					
Totals for Period														

EMPLOYEE PAYROLL RECORDS

WITHHOLDING AND DEDUCTIONS							CUMULATIVE QUARTERLY TOTALS						
Federal Tax	Social Security	Medicare	State Tax	Other	Total Deduction	Net Pay	Gross Pay	Federal Tax	Social Security	Medicare	State Tax	Other	Net Pay

FOLD

EMPLOYEE PAYROLL RECORDS

Pay Period Ending: ____________________ , 20 ____

Employee Name	Married or Single	Withholding Allowances	Hours Worked M	T	W	Th	F	Sa	Su	Total Regular Hours	Overtime Hours / Overtime Rate	Hourly Rate of Pay	Gross Pay	
Totals for Period														

EMPLOYEE PAYROLL RECORDS

WITHHOLDING AND DEDUCTIONS							CUMULATIVE QUARTERLY TOTALS						
Federal Tax	Social Security	Medicare	State Tax	Other	Total Deduction	Net Pay	Gross Pay	Federal Tax	Social Security	Medicare	State Tax	Other	Net Pay

FOLD

EMPLOYEE PAYROLL RECORDS

Pay Period Ending: ____________________ , 20 ____

Employee Name	Married or Single	Withholding Allowances	Hours Worked M	T	W	Th	F	Sa	Su	Total Regular Hours	Overtime Hours / Overtime Rate	Hourly Rate of Pay	Gross Pay	
Totals for Period														

EMPLOYEE PAYROLL RECORDS

WITHHOLDING AND DEDUCTIONS							CUMULATIVE QUARTERLY TOTALS						
Federal Tax	Social Security	Medicare	State Tax	Other	Total Deduction	Net Pay	Gross Pay	Federal Tax	Social Security	Medicare	State Tax	Other	Net Pay

FOLD

EMPLOYEE PAYROLL RECORDS

Pay Period Ending: ______________________ , 20 _____

Employee Name	Married or Single	Withholding Allowances	Hours Worked							Total Regular Hours	Overtime Hours / Overtime Rate	Hourly Rate of Pay	Gross Pay	
			M	T	W	Th	F	Sa	Su					
Totals for Period														

EMPLOYEE PAYROLL RECORDS

WITHHOLDING AND DEDUCTIONS							CUMULATIVE QUARTERLY TOTALS						
Federal Tax	Social Security	Medicare	State Tax	Other	Total Deduction	Net Pay	Gross Pay	Federal Tax	Social Security	Medicare	State Tax	Other	Net Pay

FOLD

EMPLOYEE PAYROLL RECORDS

Pay Period Ending: ______________________, 20 _____

Employee Name	Married or Single	Withholding Allowances	Hours Worked M	T	W	Th	F	Sa	Su	Total Regular Hours	Overtime Hours / Overtime Rate	Hourly Rate of Pay	Gross Pay	
Totals for Period														

EMPLOYEE PAYROLL RECORDS

WITHHOLDING AND DEDUCTIONS							CUMULATIVE QUARTERLY TOTALS						
Federal Tax	Social Security	Medicare	State Tax	Other	Total Deduction	Net Pay	Gross Pay	Federal Tax	Social Security	Medicare	State Tax	Other	Net Pay

FOLD

EMPLOYEE PAYROLL RECORDS

Pay Period Ending: ____________________ , 20 ____

Employee Name	Married or Single	Withholding Allowances	Hours Worked M	T	W	Th	F	Sa	Su	Total Regular Hours	Overtime Hours / Overtime Rate	Hourly Rate of Pay	Gross Pay	
Totals for Period														

EMPLOYEE PAYROLL RECORDS

WITHHOLDING AND DEDUCTIONS							CUMULATIVE QUARTERLY TOTALS						
Federal Tax	Social Security	Medicare	State Tax	Other	Total Deduction	Net Pay	Gross Pay	Federal Tax	Social Security	Medicare	State Tax	Other	Net Pay

FOLD

EMPLOYEE PAYROLL RECORDS

Pay Period Ending: ______________________ , 20 _____

Employee Name	Married or Single	Withholding Allowances	Hours Worked: M	T	W	Th	F	Sa	Su	Total Regular Hours	Overtime Hours / Overtime Rate	Hourly Rate of Pay	Gross Pay	
Totals for Period														

EMPLOYEE PAYROLL RECORDS

WITHHOLDING AND DEDUCTIONS							CUMULATIVE QUARTERLY TOTALS						
Federal Tax	Social Security	Medicare	State Tax	Other	Total Deduction	Net Pay	Gross Pay	Federal Tax	Social Security	Medicare	State Tax	Other	Net Pay

FOLD

EMPLOYEE PAYROLL RECORDS

Pay Period Ending: ____________________ , 20 ____

Employee Name	Married or Single	Withholding Allowances	Hours Worked M	T	W	Th	F	Sa	Su	Total Regular Hours	Overtime Hours / Overtime Rate	Hourly Rate of Pay	Gross Pay	
Totals for Period														

EMPLOYEE PAYROLL RECORDS

WITHHOLDING AND DEDUCTIONS							CUMULATIVE QUARTERLY TOTALS						
Federal Tax	Social Security	Medicare	State Tax	Other	Total Deduction	Net Pay	Gross Pay	Federal Tax	Social Security	Medicare	State Tax	Other	Net Pay

FOLD

EMPLOYEE PAYROLL RECORDS

Pay Period Ending: ______________________ , 20 ____

Employee Name	Married or Single	Withholding Allowances	Hours Worked							Total Regular Hours	Overtime Hours / Overtime Rate	Hourly Rate of Pay	Gross Pay	
			M	T	W	Th	F	Sa	Su					
Totals for Period														

EMPLOYEE PAYROLL RECORDS

WITHHOLDING AND DEDUCTIONS							CUMULATIVE QUARTERLY TOTALS						
Federal Tax	Social Security	Medicare	State Tax	Other	Total Deduction	Net Pay	Gross Pay	Federal Tax	Social Security	Medicare	State Tax	Other	Net Pay

FOLD

EMPLOYEE PAYROLL RECORDS

Pay Period Ending: ______________________ , 20 _____

Employee Name	Married or Single	Withholding Allowances	Hours Worked							Total Regular Hours	Overtime Hours / Overtime Rate	Hourly Rate of Pay	Gross Pay	
			M	T	W	Th	F	Sa	Su					
Totals for Period														

EMPLOYEE PAYROLL RECORDS

WITHHOLDING AND DEDUCTIONS							CUMULATIVE QUARTERLY TOTALS						
Federal Tax	Social Security	Medicare	State Tax	Other	Total Deduction	Net Pay	Gross Pay	Federal Tax	Social Security	Medicare	State Tax	Other	Net Pay

FOLD

2nd QUARTER EMPLOYEE PAYROLL SUMMARY

Quarter Ending: ______________________ , 20 _____

Employee Name	Gross Pay	Federal Income Tax	Social Security	Medicare	State Tax	Other	Net Pay
Totals for Quarter							

2nd QUARTER PAYROLL DEPOSITORY RECORD

Month	Federal Inome Tax		Employee Share Social Security		Employer Share Social Security		Employee Share Medicare		Employer Share Medicare		Total Deposit	
Quarterly Total												
Cumulative Total												
Total Number of Employees for Quarter:												

2nd QUARTER STATE UNEMPLOYMENT CONTRIBUTION RECORD

Employee Name	Total Quarterly Net Pay		Employee Name	Total Quarterly Net Pay	
Total Net Pay for This Column			Total Net Pay for This Column		
			Total Net Pay for All Employees (both columns)		
			x State Unemployment Multiplier Rate		
			= Total Quarterly Unemployment Due		

EMPLOYEE PAYROLL RECORDS

Pay Period Ending: ______________________ , 20 ____

Employee Name	Married or Single	Withholding Allowances	Hours Worked							Total Regular Hours	Overtime Hours / Overtime Rate	Hourly Rate of Pay	Gross Pay	
			M	T	W	Th	F	Sa	Su					
Totals for Period														

EMPLOYEE PAYROLL RECORDS

WITHHOLDING AND DEDUCTIONS							CUMULATIVE QUARTERLY TOTALS						
Federal Tax	Social Security	Medicare	State Tax	Other	Total Deduction	Net Pay	Gross Pay	Federal Tax	Social Security	Medicare	State Tax	Other	Net Pay

FOLD

EMPLOYEE PAYROLL RECORDS

Pay Period Ending: ______________________ , 20 _____

Employee Name	Married or Single	Withholding Allowances	Hours Worked M	T	W	Th	F	Sa	Su	Total Regular Hours	Overtime Hours / Overtime Rate	Hourly Rate of Pay	Gross Pay	
Totals for Period														

EMPLOYEE PAYROLL RECORDS

WITHHOLDING AND DEDUCTIONS							CUMULATIVE QUARTERLY TOTALS						
Federal Tax	Social Security	Medicare	State Tax	Other	Total Deduction	Net Pay	Gross Pay	Federal Tax	Social Security	Medicare	State Tax	Other	Net Pay

FOLD

EMPLOYEE PAYROLL RECORDS

Pay Period Ending: ______________________ , 20 _____

Employee Name	Married or Single	Withholding Allowances	Hours Worked							Total Regular Hours	Overtime Hours / Overtime Rate	Hourly Rate of Pay	Gross Pay	
			M	T	W	Th	F	Sa	Su					
Totals for Period														

EMPLOYEE PAYROLL RECORDS

WITHHOLDING AND DEDUCTIONS							CUMULATIVE QUARTERLY TOTALS						
Federal Tax	Social Security	Medicare	State Tax	Other	Total Deduction	Net Pay	Gross Pay	Federal Tax	Social Security	Medicare	State Tax	Other	Net Pay

FOLD

EMPLOYEE PAYROLL RECORDS

Pay Period Ending: ______________________ , 20 _____

Employee Name	Married or Single	Withholding Allowances	Hours Worked M	T	W	Th	F	Sa	Su	Total Regular Hours	Overtime Hours / Overtime Rate	Hourly Rate of Pay	Gross Pay	
Totals for Period														

EMPLOYEE PAYROLL RECORDS

WITHHOLDING AND DEDUCTIONS							CUMULATIVE QUARTERLY TOTALS						
Federal Tax	Social Security	Medicare	State Tax	Other	Total Deduction	Net Pay	Gross Pay	Federal Tax	Social Security	Medicare	State Tax	Other	Net Pay

FOLD

EMPLOYEE PAYROLL RECORDS

Pay Period Ending: ______________________ , 20 _____

Employee Name	Married or Single	Withholding Allowances	Hours Worked							Total Regular Hours	Overtime Hours / Overtime Rate	Hourly Rate of Pay	Gross Pay	
			M	T	W	Th	F	Sa	Su					
Totals for Period														

EMPLOYEE PAYROLL RECORDS

WITHHOLDING AND DEDUCTIONS							CUMULATIVE QUARTERLY TOTALS						
Federal Tax	Social Security	Medicare	State Tax	Other	Total Deduction	Net Pay	Gross Pay	Federal Tax	Social Security	Medicare	State Tax	Other	Net Pay

FOLD

EMPLOYEE PAYROLL RECORDS

Pay Period Ending: ______________________ , 20 ____

Employee Name	Married or Single	Withholding Allowances	Hours Worked							Total Regular Hours	Overtime Hours / Overtime Rate	Hourly Rate of Pay	Gross Pay	
			M	T	W	Th	F	Sa	Su					
Totals for Period														

EMPLOYEE PAYROLL RECORDS

WITHHOLDING AND DEDUCTIONS							CUMULATIVE QUARTERLY TOTALS						
Federal Tax	Social Security	Medicare	State Tax	Other	Total Deduction	Net Pay	Gross Pay	Federal Tax	Social Security	Medicare	State Tax	Other	Net Pay

FOLD

EMPLOYEE PAYROLL RECORDS

Pay Period Ending: ______________________ , 20 _____

Employee Name	Married or Single	Withholding Allowances	Hours Worked M	T	W	Th	F	Sa	Su	Total Regular Hours	Overtime Hours / Overtime Rate	Hourly Rate of Pay	Gross Pay	
Totals for Period														

EMPLOYEE PAYROLL RECORDS

WITHHOLDING AND DEDUCTIONS							CUMULATIVE QUARTERLY TOTALS						
Federal Tax	Social Security	Medicare	State Tax	Other	Total Deduction	Net Pay	Gross Pay	Federal Tax	Social Security	Medicare	State Tax	Other	Net Pay

FOLD

EMPLOYEE PAYROLL RECORDS

Pay Period Ending: ____________________ , 20 ____

Employee Name	Married or Single	Withholding Allowances	Hours Worked							Total Regular Hours	Overtime Hours / Overtime Rate	Hourly Rate of Pay	Gross Pay	
			M	T	W	Th	F	Sa	Su					
Totals for Period														

EMPLOYEE PAYROLL RECORDS

WITHHOLDING AND DEDUCTIONS							CUMULATIVE QUARTERLY TOTALS						
Federal Tax	Social Security	Medicare	State Tax	Other	Total Deduction	Net Pay	Gross Pay	Federal Tax	Social Security	Medicare	State Tax	Other	Net Pay

FOLD

EMPLOYEE PAYROLL RECORDS

Pay Period Ending: ______________________ , 20 _____

Employee Name	Married or Single	Withholding Allowances	Hours Worked							Total Regular Hours	Overtime Hours / Overtime Rate	Hourly Rate of Pay	Gross Pay	
			M	T	W	Th	F	Sa	Su					
Totals for Period														

EMPLOYEE PAYROLL RECORDS

WITHHOLDING AND DEDUCTIONS							CUMULATIVE QUARTERLY TOTALS						
Federal Tax	Social Security	Medicare	State Tax	Other	Total Deduction	Net Pay	Gross Pay	Federal Tax	Social Security	Medicare	State Tax	Other	Net Pay

FOLD

EMPLOYEE PAYROLL RECORDS

Pay Period Ending: ______________________ , 20 _____

Employee Name	Married or Single	Withholding Allowances	Hours Worked							Total Regular Hours	Overtime Hours / Overtime Rate	Hourly Rate of Pay	Gross Pay	
			M	T	W	Th	F	Sa	Su					
Totals for Period														

EMPLOYEE PAYROLL RECORDS

WITHHOLDING AND DEDUCTIONS							CUMULATIVE QUARTERLY TOTALS						
Federal Tax	Social Security	Medicare	State Tax	Other	Total Deduction	Net Pay	Gross Pay	Federal Tax	Social Security	Medicare	State Tax	Other	Net Pay

FOLD

EMPLOYEE PAYROLL RECORDS

Pay Period Ending: ______________________ , 20 _____

Employee Name	Married or Single	Withholding Allowances	Hours Worked M	T	W	Th	F	Sa	Su	Total Regular Hours	Overtime Hours / Overtime Rate	Hourly Rate of Pay	Gross Pay	
Totals for Period														

EMPLOYEE PAYROLL RECORDS

WITHHOLDING AND DEDUCTIONS							CUMULATIVE QUARTERLY TOTALS						
Federal Tax	Social Security	Medicare	State Tax	Other	Total Deduction	Net Pay	Gross Pay	Federal Tax	Social Security	Medicare	State Tax	Other	Net Pay

FOLD

EMPLOYEE PAYROLL RECORDS

Pay Period Ending: ______________________ , 20 _____

Employee Name	Married or Single	Withholding Allowances	Hours Worked M	T	W	Th	F	Sa	Su	Total Regular Hours	Overtime Hours / Overtime Rate	Hourly Rate of Pay	Gross Pay	
Totals for Period														

EMPLOYEE PAYROLL RECORDS

WITHHOLDING AND DEDUCTIONS							CUMULATIVE QUARTERLY TOTALS						
Federal Tax	Social Security	Medicare	State Tax	Other	Total Deduction	Net Pay	Gross Pay	Federal Tax	Social Security	Medicare	State Tax	Other	Net Pay

FOLD

EMPLOYEE PAYROLL RECORDS

Pay Period Ending: ______________________ , 20 _____

Employee Name	Married or Single	Withholding Allowances	Hours Worked							Total Regular Hours	Overtime Hours / Overtime Rate	Hourly Rate of Pay	Gross Pay	
			M	T	W	Th	F	Sa	Su					
Totals for Period														

EMPLOYEE PAYROLL RECORDS

WITHHOLDING AND DEDUCTIONS								CUMULATIVE QUARTERLY TOTALS						
Federal Tax	Social Security	Medicare	State Tax	Other	Total Deduction	Net Pay		Gross Pay	Federal Tax	Social Security	Medicare	State Tax	Other	Net Pay

FOLD

EMPLOYEE PAYROLL RECORDS

Pay Period Ending: ______________________ , 20 _____

Employee Name	Married or Single	Withholding Allowances	Hours Worked M	T	W	Th	F	Sa	Su	Total Regular Hours	Overtime Hours / Overtime Rate	Hourly Rate of Pay	Gross Pay	
Totals for Period														

EMPLOYEE PAYROLL RECORDS

WITHHOLDING AND DEDUCTIONS							CUMULATIVE QUARTERLY TOTALS						
Federal Tax	Social Security	Medicare	State Tax	Other	Total Deduction	Net Pay	Gross Pay	Federal Tax	Social Security	Medicare	State Tax	Other	Net Pay

FOLD

3rd QUARTER EMPLOYEE PAYROLL SUMMARY

Quarter Ending: ______________________ , 20 _____

Employee Name	Gross Pay		Federal Income Tax		Social Security		Medicare		State Tax		Other		Net Pay	
Totals for Quarter														

3rd QUARTER PAYROLL DEPOSITORY RECORD

Month	Federal Inome Tax	Employee Share Social Security	Employer Share Social Security	Employee Share Medicare	Employer Share Medicare	Total Deposit
Quarterly Total						
Cumulative Total						
Total Number of Employees for Quarter:						

3rd QUARTER STATE UNEMPLOYMENT CONTRIBUTION RECORD

Employee Name	Total Quarterly Net Pay	Employee Name	Total Quarterly Net Pay
Total Net Pay for This Column		Total Net Pay for This Column	
		Total Net Pay for All Employees (both columns)	
		x State Unemployment Multiplier Rate	
		= Total Quarterly Unemployment Due	

EMPLOYEE PAYROLL RECORDS

Pay Period Ending: ______________________ , 20 _____

Employee Name	Married or Single	Withholding Allowances	Hours Worked							Total Regular Hours	Overtime Hours / Overtime Rate	Hourly Rate of Pay	Gross Pay	
			M	T	W	Th	F	Sa	Su					
Totals for Period														

EMPLOYEE PAYROLL RECORDS

WITHHOLDING AND DEDUCTIONS							CUMULATIVE QUARTERLY TOTALS						
Federal Tax	Social Security	Medicare	State Tax	Other	Total Deduction	Net Pay	Gross Pay	Federal Tax	Social Security	Medicare	State Tax	Other	Net Pay

FOLD

EMPLOYEE PAYROLL RECORDS

Pay Period Ending: ______________________ , 20 _____

Employee Name	Married or Single	Withholding Allowances	Hours Worked							Total Regular Hours	Overtime Hours / Overtime Rate	Hourly Rate of Pay	Gross Pay	
			M	T	W	Th	F	Sa	Su					
Totals for Period														

EMPLOYEE PAYROLL RECORDS

WITHHOLDING AND DEDUCTIONS							CUMULATIVE QUARTERLY TOTALS						
Federal Tax	Social Security	Medicare	State Tax	Other	Total Deduction	Net Pay	Gross Pay	Federal Tax	Social Security	Medicare	State Tax	Other	Net Pay

FOLD

EMPLOYEE PAYROLL RECORDS

Pay Period Ending: ______________________ , 20 _____

Employee Name	Married or Single	Withholding Allowances	Hours Worked M	T	W	Th	F	Sa	Su	Total Regular Hours	Overtime Hours / Overtime Rate	Hourly Rate of Pay	Gross Pay	
Totals for Period														

EMPLOYEE PAYROLL RECORDS

WITHHOLDING AND DEDUCTIONS							CUMULATIVE QUARTERLY TOTALS						
Federal Tax	Social Security	Medicare	State Tax	Other	Total Deduction	Net Pay	Gross Pay	Federal Tax	Social Security	Medicare	State Tax	Other	Net Pay

FOLD

EMPLOYEE PAYROLL RECORDS

Pay Period Ending: ______________________ , 20 _____

Employee Name	Married or Single	Withholding Allowances	Hours Worked M	T	W	Th	F	Sa	Su	Total Regular Hours	Overtime Hours / Overtime Rate	Hourly Rate of Pay	Gross Pay	
Totals for Period														

EMPLOYEE PAYROLL RECORDS

WITHHOLDING AND DEDUCTIONS							CUMULATIVE QUARTERLY TOTALS						
Federal Tax	Social Security	Medicare	State Tax	Other	Total Deduction	Net Pay	Gross Pay	Federal Tax	Social Security	Medicare	State Tax	Other	Net Pay

FOLD

EMPLOYEE PAYROLL RECORDS

Pay Period Ending: ______________________ , 20 _____

Employee Name	Married or Single	Withholding Allowances	Hours Worked							Total Regular Hours	Overtime Hours / Overtime Rate	Hourly Rate of Pay	Gross Pay	
			M	T	W	Th	F	Sa	Su					
Totals for Period														

EMPLOYEE PAYROLL RECORDS

WITHHOLDING AND DEDUCTIONS							CUMULATIVE QUARTERLY TOTALS						
Federal Tax	Social Security	Medicare	State Tax	Other	Total Deduction	Net Pay	Gross Pay	Federal Tax	Social Security	Medicare	State Tax	Other	Net Pay

FOLD

EMPLOYEE PAYROLL RECORDS

Pay Period Ending: ______________________ , 20 ____

Employee Name	Married or Single	Withholding Allowances	Hours Worked							Total Regular Hours	Overtime Hours / Overtime Rate	Hourly Rate of Pay	Gross Pay	
			M	T	W	Th	F	Sa	Su					
Totals for Period														

EMPLOYEE PAYROLL RECORDS

WITHHOLDING AND DEDUCTIONS							CUMULATIVE QUARTERLY TOTALS						
Federal Tax	Social Security	Medicare	State Tax	Other	Total Deduction	Net Pay	Gross Pay	Federal Tax	Social Security	Medicare	State Tax	Other	Net Pay

FOLD

EMPLOYEE PAYROLL RECORDS

Pay Period Ending: ______________________ , 20 _____

Employee Name	Married or Single	Withholding Allowances	Hours Worked							Total Regular Hours	Overtime Hours / Overtime Rate	Hourly Rate of Pay	Gross Pay	
			M	T	W	Th	F	Sa	Su					
Totals for Period														

EMPLOYEE PAYROLL RECORDS

WITHHOLDING AND DEDUCTIONS							CUMULATIVE QUARTERLY TOTALS						
Federal Tax	Social Security	Medicare	State Tax	Other	Total Deduction	Net Pay	Gross Pay	Federal Tax	Social Security	Medicare	State Tax	Other	Net Pay

FOLD

EMPLOYEE PAYROLL RECORDS

Pay Period Ending: ______________________ , 20 _____

Employee Name	Married or Single	Withholding Allowances	Hours Worked M	T	W	Th	F	Sa	Su	Total Regular Hours	Overtime Hours / Overtime Rate	Hourly Rate of Pay	Gross Pay	
Totals for Period														

EMPLOYEE PAYROLL RECORDS

WITHHOLDING AND DEDUCTIONS							CUMULATIVE QUARTERLY TOTALS						
Federal Tax	Social Security	Medicare	State Tax	Other	Total Deduction	Net Pay	Gross Pay	Federal Tax	Social Security	Medicare	State Tax	Other	Net Pay

FOLD

EMPLOYEE PAYROLL RECORDS

Pay Period Ending: ______________________ , 20 _____

Employee Name	Married or Single	Withholding Allowances	Hours Worked							Total Regular Hours	Overtime Hours / Overtime Rate	Hourly Rate of Pay	Gross Pay	
			M	T	W	Th	F	Sa	Su					
Totals for Period														

EMPLOYEE PAYROLL RECORDS

WITHHOLDING AND DEDUCTIONS							CUMULATIVE QUARTERLY TOTALS						
Federal Tax	Social Security	Medicare	State Tax	Other	Total Deduction	Net Pay	Gross Pay	Federal Tax	Social Security	Medicare	State Tax	Other	Net Pay

FOLD

EMPLOYEE PAYROLL RECORDS

Pay Period Ending: ______________________ , 20 _____

Employee Name	Married or Single	Withholding Allowances	Hours Worked M	T	W	Th	F	Sa	Su	Total Regular Hours	Overtime Hours / Overtime Rate	Hourly Rate of Pay	Gross Pay
Totals for Period													

EMPLOYEE PAYROLL RECORDS

WITHHOLDING AND DEDUCTIONS							CUMULATIVE QUARTERLY TOTALS						
Federal Tax	Social Security	Medicare	State Tax	Other	Total Deduction	Net Pay	Gross Pay	Federal Tax	Social Security	Medicare	State Tax	Other	Net Pay

FOLD

EMPLOYEE PAYROLL RECORDS

Pay Period Ending: ______________________ , 20 _____

Employee Name	Married or Single	Withholding Allowances	Hours Worked							Total Regular Hours	Overtime Hours / Overtime Rate	Hourly Rate of Pay	Gross Pay	
			M	T	W	Th	F	Sa	Su					
Totals for Period														

EMPLOYEE PAYROLL RECORDS

WITHHOLDING AND DEDUCTIONS							CUMULATIVE QUARTERLY TOTALS						
Federal Tax	Social Security	Medicare	State Tax	Other	Total Deduction	Net Pay	Gross Pay	Federal Tax	Social Security	Medicare	State Tax	Other	Net Pay

FOLD

EMPLOYEE PAYROLL RECORDS

Pay Period Ending: ______________________ , 20 _____

Employee Name	Married or Single	Withholding Allowances	Hours Worked							Total Regular Hours	Overtime Hours / Overtime Rate	Hourly Rate of Pay	Gross Pay	
			M	T	W	Th	F	Sa	Su					
Totals for Period														

EMPLOYEE PAYROLL RECORDS

WITHHOLDING AND DEDUCTIONS							CUMULATIVE QUARTERLY TOTALS						
Federal Tax	Social Security	Medicare	State Tax	Other	Total Deduction	Net Pay	Gross Pay	Federal Tax	Social Security	Medicare	State Tax	Other	Net Pay

FOLD

EMPLOYEE PAYROLL RECORDS

Pay Period Ending: ______________________ , 20 _____

Employee Name	Married or Single	Withholding Allowances	Hours Worked M	T	W	Th	F	Sa	Su	Total Regular Hours	Overtime Hours / Overtime Rate	Hourly Rate of Pay	Gross Pay	
Totals for Period														

EMPLOYEE PAYROLL RECORDS

WITHHOLDING AND DEDUCTIONS							CUMULATIVE QUARTERLY TOTALS						
Federal Tax	Social Security	Medicare	State Tax	Other	Total Deduction	Net Pay	Gross Pay	Federal Tax	Social Security	Medicare	State Tax	Other	Net Pay

FOLD

EMPLOYEE PAYROLL RECORDS

Pay Period Ending: ______________________ , 20 _____

Employee Name	Married or Single	Withholding Allowances	Hours Worked M	T	W	Th	F	Sa	Su	Total Regular Hours	Overtime Hours / Overtime Rate	Hourly Rate of Pay	Gross Pay	
Totals for Period														

EMPLOYEE PAYROLL RECORDS

WITHHOLDING AND DEDUCTIONS							CUMULATIVE QUARTERLY TOTALS						
Federal Tax	Social Security	Medicare	State Tax	Other	Total Deduction	Net Pay	Gross Pay	Federal Tax	Social Security	Medicare	State Tax	Other	Net Pay

FOLD

4th QUARTER AND ANNUAL EMPLOYEE PAYROLL SUMMARY

Quarter Ending: ______________________ , 20 ____

Employee Name	Gross Pay	Federal Income Tax	Social Security	Medicare	State Tax	Other	Net Pay
Totals for 4th Quarter							
Totals for 3rd Quarter							
Totals for 2nd Quarter							
Totals for 1st Quarter							
Totals for Year							

4th QUARTER AND ANNUAL PAYROLL DEPOSITORY RECORD

Month	Federal Inome Tax	Employee Share Social Security	Employer Share Social Security	Employee Share Medicare	Employer Share Medicare	Total Deposit
4th Quarter Total						
3rd Quarter Total						
2nd Quarter Total						
1st Quarter Total						
Annual Total						
Total Number of Employees for Quarter:						

4th QUARTER AND ANNUAL STATE UNEMPLOYMENT CONTRIBUTION RECORD

Employee Name	Total Quarterly Net Pay	Employee Name	Total Quarterly Net Pay
Total Net Pay for This Column		Total Net Pay for This Column	
		Total Net Pay for All Employees (both columns)	
		x State Unemployment Multiplier Rate	
		= Total 4th Quarter Unemployment Due	
		+ Total 3rd Quarter Unemployment Paid	
		+ Total 2nd Quarter Unemployment Paid	
		+ Total 1st Quarter Unemployment Paid	
		= Total Annual	

★ Nova Publishing Company ★

Small Business and Consumer Legal Books and Software

Small Business Made Simple Series		
Small Business Payroll Systems Simplified		
ISBN 0-935755-55-1	Book only	$14.95
Small Business Bookkeeping Systems Simplified		
ISBN 0-935755-74-8	Book only	$14.95
Small Business Accounting Simplified (3rd Edition)		
ISBN 0-935755-91-8	Book only	$22.95
Law Made Simple Series		
Basic Wills Simplified		
ISBN 0-935755-90-X	Book only	$22.95
ISBN 0-935755-89-6	Book w/Forms-on-CD	$28.95
Divorce Agreements Simplified		
ISBN 0-935755-87-X	Book only	$24.95
ISBN 0-935755-86-1	Book w/Forms-on-CD	$29.95
Living Wills Simplified		
ISBN 0-935755-52-7	Book only	$22.95
ISBN 0-935755-50-0	Book w/Forms-on-CD	$28.95
Living Trusts Simplified		
ISBN 0-935755-53-5	Book only	$22.95
ISBN 0-935755-51-9	Book w/Forms-on-CD	$28.95
Personal Legal Forms Simplified (available late 2003)		
ISBN 0-935755-97-7	Book w/Forms-on-CD	$27.95
Small Business Library Series		
The Complete Book of Small Business Legal Forms (3rd Edition)		
ISBN 0-935755-84-5	Book w/Forms-on-CD	$24.95
Incorporate Your Business: The National Corporation Kit (3rd Edition)		
ISBN 0-935755-88-8	Book w/Forms-on-CD	$24.95
The Complete Book of Small Business Management Forms		
ISBN 0-935755-56-X	Book w/Forms-on-CD	$24.95
Small Business Start-up Series		
C-Corporations: Small Business Start-up Kit		
ISBN 0-935755-78-0	Book w/Forms-on-CD	$24.95
S-Corporations: Small Business Start-up Kit		
ISBN 0-935755-77-2	Book w/Forms-on-CD	$24.95
Partnerships: Small Business Start-up Kit		
ISBN 0-935755-75-6	Book w/Forms-on-CD	$24.95
Limited Liability Company: Small Business Start-up Kit		
ISBN 0-935755-76-4	Book w/Forms-on-CD	$24.95
Sole Proprietorship: Small Business Start-up Kit		
ISBN 0-935755-79-9	Book w/Forms-on-CD	$24.95
Legal Self-Help Series		
Debt Free: The National Bankruptcy Kit (2nd Edition)		
ISBN 0-935755-62-4	Book only	$19.95
The Complete Book of Personal Legal Forms (3rd Edition)		
ISBN 0-935755-92-6	Book w/Forms-on-CD	$24.95
Divorce Yourself: The National No-Fault Divorce Kit (5th Edition)		
ISBN 0-935755-93-4	Book only	$24.95
ISBN 0-935755-94-2	Book w/Forms-on-CD	$34.95
Prepare Your Own Will: The National Will Kit (5th Edition)		
ISBN 0-935755-72-1	Book only	$17.95
ISBN 0-935755-73-X	Book w/Forms-on-CD	$27.95

★ Ordering Information ★

Distributed by:
National Book Network
4720 Boston Way
Lanham MD 20706

Shipping/handling: $4.50 for first book or disk and $.75 for each additional
Phone orders with Visa/MC: (800) 462-6420
Fax orders with Visa/MC: (800) 338-4550
Internet: www.novapublishing.com